Fallow Field

Fallow Field

Poems

Scott Edward Anderson

Aldrich Press

Cover photograph: © *1997 Joshua Sheldon*

ISBN-13: 978-0615867359

Aldrich Press
24600 Mountain Avenue, Suite 35
Hemet, California 92544

For Samantha—fully, completely, and absolutely.

Acknowledgments

Abyss & Apex: "An 'Unkindness' of Ravens" (April 2010)

Alaska Quarterly Review: "Naming" (Summer 2001)

American Poetry Review: "Intelligent Design" (July/August 2008)

Anon: "Midnight Sun" (Spring 2010)

Blueline: "Dead Red Wing," "Fallow Field" and "Opportunity" (Summer 2005)

Bolts of Silk: "Cultivating (Preserving)" (2010)

The Cortland Review: "Osage Moon" (May 2002)

CrossConnect: "Indwelling" and "Running" (Fall 2000)

Earth's Daughters: "Bread" and "Reckoning" (Winter 1999; Winter 1997)

Elegant Thorn Review: "Healing" (Spring 2007)

Harrisburg Review: "Body in Motion" (Spring 1999)

Isotope: "Confusing Fall Warblers" (Spring 2004)

Kimera: "Saudade" and "Salt" (Summer 1999)

La Petite Zine: "Two Views" and "Hoarfrost & Rime" (Summer 2001)

The Nebraska Review: "Black Angus, Winter," "Deserted Sheep," and "Granite" (Spring/Summer 1997)

Philadelphia Stories: "Spartina" (December 2004)

Piedmont Literary Review: "The Vermont Quartet" (Winter 1995-96)

Poetic Mind Set: "Second Skin: A Sestina" (April 2011)

Terrain: A Journal of the Built and Natural Environments: "Redshifting," "Shapeshifting," "Mapping," "Ten-Legged Polar Bear," "Day of the Earth, Night of the Locusts" and "Hope Against Hope" (March 2005; March 2002; September 2000; Summer 2003, respectively)

"Second Skin" appeared in *The Incredible Sestina Anthology* published by Write Bloody Publishing, 2013.

"The Poet Gene" received an honorable mention in the 2011 ESRC Genomics Forum Poetry Competition co-sponsored by the Economic and Social Research Council's Genomics Network and the Scottish Poetry Library of Edinburgh.

"Calvin's Story" and "Redbud & Pitbull" appeared in the anthology, *Dogs Singing: A Tribute* published by Salmon Poetry, 2010.

"Becoming" appeared on a glass wall display at the Millay Colony for the Arts, 30th Anniversary Exhibit, Albany International Airport Gallery, in a juried show (selected by John Ashbery), January-August 2004.

"Black Angus, Winter," "Deserted Sheep," and "Granite" won the *Nebraska Review* Award, 1997.

"Gleanings" appeared in the anthology *Under a Gull's Wing: Poems & Photographs of the Jersey Shore* published by Down the Shore Press, 1997.

"Benj. A. Thresher Builds Logging Sleds in Barnet, VT" appeared in the anthology *Fire Readings: The Shakespeare & Co Fire Benefit Readings* published by Frank Books, 1993.

The author wishes to thank Alison Hawthorne Deming, Donald Hall, Robert Hass, Colette Inez, the late Walter Pavlich, Andrea Ross, Gary Snyder, and Karen Swenson for reading poems in this volume and offering helpful responses. Grateful acknowledgment also goes to the Millay Colony for the Arts and the Concordia Foundation for time and space to complete some of the poems in this manuscript. He also wishes to thank the many friends, mentors, colleagues, and family members who accompanied him on the journey to this book

Table of Contents

Fallow Field

I.

Fallow Field

The old car is there,
where she left it,
out by the old shed,
breeding rust—obscured
from the roadway by the rye grass
that grows up all around.
Long triangular tentacles
blowing and bending
in the hot breeze, as
sunlight filters
through gathering clouds.
By now the grass has worked
up into the engine block.
The car
is planted now,
in this fallow field,
awaiting bulldozers.
They call this grass
"poverty grain," and there's
no small comfort in the fact
that it's as tolerant
of poor soils
as she was of her marriage.
On the day she left,
she packed her whole life
into an old grip: clothing,
framed photographs
of the children, her parents,
the salt cellar she'd bought
on her honeymoon in Rome.
While packing, she'd given
pause that her whole life

had become so
portable, where once there'd
been permanence. And now,
she blows and bends—
rye grass on a midsummer afternoon.

Naming

The way a name lingers in the snow
when traced by hand.
The way angels are made in snow,
all body down,
arms moving from side to ear to side to ear—
a whisper, a pause;
slight, melting hesitation—

The pause in the hand as it moves
over a name carved in black granite.
The *Chuck, Chuck, Chuck,*
of great-tailed grackles
at southern coastal marshes,
or the way magpies repeat,
Meg, Meg, Meg—

The way the rib cage of a whale
resembles the architecture of I. M. Pei.
The way two names on a page
separated by thousands of lines,
pages, bookshelves, miles, can be connected.
The way wind hums through cord grass;
rain on bluestem, on mesquite—

The sandpiper's tremble
as it skitters over tidal mudflats,
tracking names in the wet silt,
silt that has been building
since Foreman lost to Ali,
since Troy fell—building until
we forget names altogether—

The way children, who know only
syllables endlessly repeated,
connect one moment to the next
humming, humming, humming—
The way magpies connect branches
into thickets for their nesting—

Curve of thumb caressing
the letters of a loved one's name
on the printed page, connecting
each letter with a trace of oil
from fingerprint to fingerprint,
again and again and again—

Black Angus, Winter

I.

The angus rap their noses
on the ice—
fat, gentle fists
rooting water
from the trough.
They kick up clods of dirt
as a madrigal of shudders
ripples their hides.

II.

The barn needs painting,
it's chipped like ice
from an ice-cutter's axe.
The fence also needs work,
posts leaning, wire slack.
The Angus keep still—
they're smarter than we think,
know all about electricity.

III.

I cross the barnyard
on my way back from the pond,
ice skates keeping time
against the small of my back.
The sting of the air
is tempered by the heat of manure.
Through the barn door:
Veal calf jabbing at her mother's udder.

Deserted Sheep

Lambs, jostled, *forgive*
    the wolf, break
     its taste in lamb
into a toddler's gallop,
bumping headlong

into thick-piled ewes—
lanolin slicking their noses, as
they stumble on the fescue
dotting the valley,
a pointillist's landscape.

No shepherd, no sheep dog,
no gate to enter; a small,
orange plastic snow fence,
neatly staked at four corners
with steel posts,
gives form to the sheepcote.

The last ounce of sun
a violet tremor *the wolf*
    forgives, lingering
along the western ridge,
    the shepherd's fear
returning to the valley.

A ram, brown and flocculent,
secures a silent corner
of the fold—eyes intent
upon a slow-moving shadow.

Granite

"All night the eyes of deer shine for an instant..." Kenneth Rexroth

Cleansed by burns, their headpieces
have outrageous symmetry.
Snow bunting at the birdfeeder: Alighting, but
knocked-away by nervous sparrows
two birch stands from the hillside.

Splitting wood,
as trees shift their shadows
in the weight of winter.
It's easy to get lost in these woods,
yet be sure of design.
As eyes of deer vanish into the feldspar,
muscles aching, sweat soaking shirt.

The oak door to the yellow house
opens with a louder noise
than that with which it shuts,
belying its hundred years.
And inside, the hearth is tested,
faces, around the granite,
recognized for their hypnotic gestures.

In the house, stamp down the day.
Snow from boots
melts on the granite firebreak.
The deer don't notice
                    when you've gone.

Dead Red Wing

Of your famous epaulets
only a hint
on the shoulder,
                  like a wound
opened when my
finger luffs the down,
still dappled with immaturity.
Tangy scar from thorn or thicket,
but not the end of you.

Come spring, you'd be up
in the low trees,
on telephone wires,
bowing foxtail in the marsh,
your song become vain
"Look-at-meeee...Look-at-meeee..."
Flash of red on black wing
poised to singe the eyes
trained on you,
a life-bird,
through field glasses.

In my hand you are stiff,
unrecognizable.
The woman
who brought you
to the birding group
kept you
in a Ziploc bag
in the freezer,
next to the roast
and last week's red beans.
Every evening,

when she finished her vigil
at the window,
she took you out,
rubbed your cold breast,
ruffled feathers,
sang your song.

Confusing Fall Warblers

"They changed your name from Brown to Jones, and mine from Brown to Blue..."
George Jones

Was it Hank Williams
she called the Nashville warbler,
or was it the black-throated blue?
Was it Wilson's warbler
she heard in the bog up north
chattering *chi chi chi chi chi chet chet?*

Yellow-throat or orange-crowned,
from Tennessee, Connecticut, or
Canada, the prothonotary
clerks for the vireo from Philly,
who is neither lawyer nor warbler,
but is often mistaken—

Was it the hooded warbler
that startled her from the thicket,
or mourning warbler's balancing notes
chirry chirry, chorry chorry,
that made her cock her head
to listen for its secret?

And tell me, tell me truly,
was it only
that sad country song
playing on the car radio
that made her cry?

(After Roger Tory Peterson's *A Field Guide to the Birds,* plate 52)

Spartina

Chincoteague, Virginia Eastern Shore

Herring gull dragged from the cord grass by a feral, bay cat,
who drops the sputtering gull under a tree.

The gull's left wing and leg are broken—right wing thrashing,
body turning round a point, compass tracing a circle.

Wild chorus of gulls tracing the same circle in salt haze
only wider, concentric, thirty feet overhead.

The cat lying down in shade, making furtive stabs,
powerful paws slapping down motion.

The cat's feral, calico-covered muscles ebb and shudder
in the bay breeze, waving in wind and water.

Now she yawns indelicately, fur and feathers
lofting on the incoming tide.

The gull plants his beak in the sand,
tethered, like all of us, to fate.

Gleanings

Ocean Grove, NJ

Look at the two of them, bent
to the early morning tide.
Culling glass from the gritty surf.
Strange and wonderful alchemists,
who search for the elusive blue
of medicine bottles, caressing
emerald imitators from "Old Latrobe,"
or amber sea urchins
left there like whelks at low tide.

They discard broken bits of crockery,
forsaken jetsam of the sands.
Beach glass is opaque
with a false clarity:
Polished by sand and sea,
the edges don't cut
like our lives, lived elsewhere,
out beyond the last sandbar,
where plate tectonics rule the waves.

Hope Against Hope

My mind is a slate gray sky about to open up over the capitol.
Electricity grounds itself to Rhode Island's terminal moraine,
and Narragansett Bay is alive with activity.
Providence is like a tree, grafted to increase yield:
the scion of this hybrid is *Freedom* and the stock, *Hope*.
Did Roger Williams have this in mind, on the day
he was expelled from Massachusetts Bay Colony
and exiled to "Rogue's Island?"

My mind is bent to the future
like a fly buzzing against a table lamp,
guided by some unknown power to the light.
Spruce-trees freckle Rhode Island's low hills,
like "Indians" on horseback overlooking a settlement
in some old western. *Years are not a life*,
trees come down with heavy snow or summer storms,
others are cut to fuel fires in cast-iron stoves,
or are cleared for houses on subdivided acres.

Providence is an article of faith
as much as of divinity. Maybe a life is determined
in the balance of past, present, and future.
Providence, in the immutable language of trees:
Tulip-trees heavy-laden with their "magnolia" blossoms;
post oaks, twisted and stunted, like worried warriors;
ash, hickory, hope; willow, red spruce, blood;
poplar, pine, providence; sandy loam, eelgrass, freedom;
arrow-arum, water weed, Wampanoag; hope against hope.

II.

Salt

Blood, leached of redness,
in a confluence of tears.

Sweat of a lover,
in evaporating recline.

Dry bones and breath
—the taste of dreaming.

Sargassum drifting
in a pelagic wave.

Body in Motion

Sinew, charge, and light—
muscle etching a concourse of air,
heat and flutter
thrum of pump house,
or pop of ligaments
snapping shut.
So quiet the fabric of skin,
taut, slack then taut again.
Flex and stretch with single purpose,
gauge of weight and distribution.
Placement of form becoming new,
as in never accomplished before,
as in a position to be named later.
Sublime, the arc of breath:
ether of air, atom, matter—
particles colluding in space.

Saudade

"I feel beliefs that I do not hold. I am ravished by passions I repudiate."
Fernando Pessoa

We're surrounded by people
who sentimentalize collegiate life,
swoon over first marriages,
or live in days gone by.
The Portuguese have a word for it,
saudade, a longing for lost things.

For myself, I have fond memories
of houses in New England
(where my childhood
blossomed, disappeared);
of a life of the mind.

But what I long for
is the old cherry tree,
in front of our home
—we were newly wed—
how it dashed its branches
against our roof.

Opportunity

A wasp wrestles all day
with the false freedom
of a window pane.

Scaling the glass, then slipping
down, buzzing the cracked paint
of the old window frame.

As if thrumming wings faster
will pull it closer to the blossom,
just beyond its reach.

So determined in its struggle
to get in, to wrest pollen from
the exotic flower on the other side.

A spider sets its dinner table
in the corner of the pane—

Day of the Earth, Night of the Locusts

Owlspent, our days are numbered,
we count them in their passing
with eyes closed, and night comes
easily to those who sleep
with blinded eyes wide open.
And double-talk is all we get
from those whose hands hold fate.

In the larkspur
at the grove's end,
pagan by rite,
we suss the folly of symbolism
and awaken
to the owl's haunting.

Eyespeak, our gods implore us
to look beyond our smugness.
And there, we find
our temples
are burdened by wreckage
and our own misdeeding.

Do we good justice by our actions?
Uneducated stewards, electable
guardians of a lackluster paradise.
The apples bruise to the grasses,
blades fat as a night-sweat.
The others have little say,
our own descent is a cant—

The question is:
Can we be faithful stewards
when there is no bounty?

Two Views

"Ya know, I wouldn't fall a tree with them in it. But I sure like to tell them that. I just get lippy. I get fired up...you tell them anything."
   Arlington Earl "A.E." Ammons

        I.
How tall you are,
longer than my life here
among these blades and oil.
Felled, you might be half
the length of a football field,
yet I can't get inside of you.
Somewhere in there
past the cambium,
is a beam so straight
it could support my two kids
about to enter college.
                        Dead–standing,
you're a condo complex
for invertebrates.
Heartwood shipped overseas,
waste wood pulped
then glued together again,
you'll make a sturdy chair.
You are mine. Without me,
you are nothing; I made you useful.
If I leave you, you too will leave.

        II.
I can hear you breathing,
like hundred–year–old men
who've counted their lives in cigarette packs—
Your phloem constricts,
there are knots in your shoulders
no massage could work out.

36

My hands are stained guilty
with cadmium red paint, as
I brand the yellow CATS
on their hind-quarters,
feed sugar into their gas tanks
to stall their insatiable appetites.
Unlike horses, they don't
nibble my fingers.
We are leveled in leveling you.
You have stood for ages;
no one alive has seen you
in your youth.

The Glimmerglass

Being a sequence of stanzas concerning Lake Otsego ("The Glimmerglass"),
which forms the headwaters of the Susquehanna River, in Cooperstown,
New York

The bats skim
over the evening ripples
of Lake Otsego.
In their blind minds
they see reflection.
    o

The curious mountains
meld with their image
in the looking-glass.
In their obvious stillness
they decline comment.
    o

Lime-colored duckweed
splays patterns
on the marsh water,
red sky corn-dancing
on Sydney's Hill.
    o

The sun sets
behind the Webster Farm.
As it falls deeper, clouds pass in the haze.
Speckled cows, curious sheep
freckle the hillside.
    o

Freshly harvested,
farmer Webster's hay
will be baled the following day—
the secrets of summer heat,
revealed & thoughtful.
    o

The moon rises
from behind the back
of the Sleeping Lion,
turns her face
to the glimmering star.

○

Dark, silent wood
balancing the four corners
of this room—
Through the window,
see the falling water.

○

Long-awaited
tenacity of rain,
giving way to a sun-doused
day of departure.
Farewells, *soaked sleeves*.

The Vermont Quartet

I. Benj. A. Thresher Builds Logging Sleds in Barnet, Vermont

He culls the perfect heartwood from a log,
as if the runners came from grace divined,
each sled he makes will have no analogue.
Some days he longs to hang it all, unwind,
but to his tiresome work he stays inclined.
The sleds he makes seem anxious for the snow,
providing livelihood, or peace of mind
for people in the valley there below.
Toil and trial, he works with little show,
and plies his craft attentive and alone.
In confidence, his workshop light aglow,
he knows a cornmeal pudding waits at home.
When night's etude lends solace to his days,
he'll sleep, preferring pudding to all praise.

II. Imagining Memphremagog

We've planned to see her every year
since first we heard her dulcet tones:
        The serpentine lake with shores of stone,
where French is spoke in rasping hues

        and snaps the roofs of frozen mouths,
reminds us she starts in old Quebec.
        The rain or wind has kept us south,
and west, in Burlington, or further

outside of Starksboro, *de rigueur.*
It seems a long way, there to here.

But I imagine Memphremagog,
in my mind's own birch bark canoe;

The Abnaki as our guides, we trust
she'll be there on our northward thrust.

III. THE COUNTRY OF MISGIVINGS

Hermit crabs, we move from place to place
dwelling in other's houses not as guests.
Less welcomed by the owners, face to face,
our lifestyle leaves us timid soloists.
As quickly as we think, we lose perspective,
that gets us into trouble with the law.
So we discard the house we thought protective;
never learning is our one great tragic flaw.
Blame the country, "Its character is lacking,"
set out by foot or rail to find new lands.
Never think it's our own fault we're sent packing,
without our wits, we fly from other's hands.
Though we may never, ever know the truth,
this country of misgivings begs the proof.

IV. Mt. Mansfield Dilemma

     Up near the summit we yield a chance
through nature's own delineation.
     To us, at least, a choice that is best:
Autumn behind, winter up ahead.
     The brilliant calico valley's grace,
which speaks to us of meals and bed,

     or the icy evergreen expanse,
which crops the mountain's bulging chin
     and calls into mind my two-day face.
From the coy starkmourn of alpine sedge,
     we see through Smugglers Notch up north,
to the feet of whiter mountains east,

     or west across Champlain's swirldeep
and blue Adirondack highland's mirth.
     Now we pass over the terrace steep,
that spans all this man's field's craggy edge,
     and from this place we choose our course:
To return, but not go back to earth.

Reckoning

Camel's Hump, Vermont, 4083'

I.
Your abacus of worries,
me, counting my own pace, afraid
of the one real thing
I've known in years—
Negotiating our vertiginous October,
up through birch, maple, oak, cedar, white pine;
granite rising like barnacles on a humpback.
　　　How do you stay calm?
Conceit hangs from my pack
like an extra water bottle.
I have trouble listening:
Do you want to push me over the summit,
or knock me out with a chunk of granite?
The mountain is *not* mine, I fool myself
　　　when I play the king.

II.
We get turned around, tricked by language:
The ring of civilization in "Forest City,"
or the sylvan slur of "Forestry."
The wrong trail is the one I've chosen—
And through the muddle, darkness comes,
and fourteen miles is the double of seven.
We switchback over the mountain's bulge
and bushwhack round its base,
hours multiplied by circumference.

III.
At last back at camp,
we learn to count on each other.
From the stone house meadow:
Our prankster's rising hump.
We curse and praise its witchery.
On that rock-ribbed blackberry hill
of Vermont's quiet reckoning, we
calculate the chalk silhouette
in a moonlit night's
heavy charcoal horizon.

Osage Moon

Tallgrass Prairie, Pawhuska, Oklahoma

The moon
is a soft pinprick
in a sky
so expansive
even Ursa
Major seems minor.
A dog barks
and ghost voices
echo down Indian song—
piercing the silhouetted Osage hills.
Grasses are weather-worn
and wild; wild-
flowers lie dormant—
everything abides green days.
Besides, cold weather slants
in from the north, taking the plains,
where a few days ago
hot winds came
up from the Gulf of Mexico,
fooling the dogwood,
and fires seared the earth
the color of burnt toast.
Miles, miles of dry grass
and sky
in every direction—
binding grasses,
four-color wildflowers,
and forbs pressed between pages,
tangled in bluestem.
And there, where bison stood
at noon, sheltered
by blackjack oak,

only shadows—
unruly apparitions,
under the Osage moon,
awaiting the culling
of their existence.

Midnight Sun

at approximately 59° 45' N Latitude, 154° 55' W Longitude

Each night,
I watch the sun set
over Lake Iliamna
through the willows.
How physical,
the names of willows:
Bebb and Scouler,
feltleaf, arctic, undergreen—
names ill-suited for their frail appearance.
And how palpable the story,
told by the black-capped chickadee
about the four bears who come
each night to the village,
linger for a couple of hours,
then vanish.
As the bird now vanishes
from atop the satellite dish
outside the room at Gram's B&B.
He leaves behind
a white remembrance,
which disturbs the signal
coming from Anchorage,
interrupting a program about
the formation of the Hawaiian Islands,
and sending ripples of multi-colored "snow"
swirling into TV screen volcanoes.
While back outside,
midsummer sun barely sets on the village,
angling over sparse willows
and spruce, bentgrass and sweetgale,
perhaps twinflower, although
verifying the presence of that species

may require a second look.
A second look, which the sun
will suggest, upon its return
four and one-half hours from now.
That is when the BLM surveyors will arrive
on their ATVs (whatever the weather
and whether they're foolish or clever),
to verify yesterday's measurements,
as they do each morning,
in this village of willows
and midnight sun.

An "Unkindness" of Ravens

Anchorage, Alaska

To fall asleep at night, I count ravens
from my bedroom window.
They gather in the spruce trees
at the edge of the woods,
as snow gathers dusk on its surface.
By midnight, thirty or forty
have gathered there in the oily dark.

As a group, they are called "an unkindness,"
but they are polite
and helpful to each other,
share their successes and failures
pursue joy and embrace their strength
in numbers, which is more than we can say.

Plummeting downhill, they launch into air,
as if snowboarding; flipping and spinning
— hell-bent teenagers on a half-pipe.
In more sober moments, they tell each other
where to look for food, when danger is near,
and where the good garbage is. They discuss
variable wind speeds or compare moose meat
found in the woods with that of roadside kills.

They can be graceful on the wing—Naiads
of the air—or clumsy and indelicate,
half-eaten bagels dangling from black beaks.
Dusk comes later and later these evenings,
and morning arrives sooner, winter almost over.
Come Easter, the ravens will be gone.
Ravens prefer dead things remain dead.

The Ten-legged Polar Bear

"You westerners don't understand consensus. You think it means mutual
agreement. Consensus means mutual understanding."
    Gregory Anelon, Sr., Yup'ik elder

Ten legs are better than two
only if they work together—

when all five legs on one side
and all five legs on the other side

move in concert like a sled runner,
the Qupqugiaq moves smoothly,

but if the legs get tangled up
and one leg trips up another,

then another trips another,
the whole bear comes crashing

down; it takes a lot to get
a ten-legged polar bear upright

and get it moving again—

(Qupqugiaq: a legendary ten-footed polar bear described by the Inupiaq of
Alaska's Arctic North Slope)

Hoarfrost & Rime

Hoarfrost and rime will soon embrace
devil's club, spruce, and kinnikinnik,
sharpening autumn colors in fading light.
Now the last blueberries, overlooked
by dozing bears, await Raven's bidding;
now tundra swans gabble and *woo-ga-loo,*
as the sun lowers its angle over river and tundra,
over those of us who call the "Great Land" home.

Disappearance

In the distance we see what appears to be floating sea-ice,
calved from ragged ice-edge, only it's rounded, tensile,
    mammalian—

Hollow points of light emanating from softly echoing,
transparent follicles; then a broad back surfaces, inanimate—

"Oh my god, it's a bear!" someone shouts, pointing
to a floating carcass now seen clearly: not sea-ice,

but sea-*bear*—*Urus maritimus*—dead-man's floating
miles and miles from the nearest shore,

face staring deep beneath the surface, massive front paws
spent from stretching, from reaching for ice-edge,

exhausted from swimming panicky circles,
finding only heavy arctic seawater, viscous oil, adrenaline ooze.

Think of a fight-weary heavyweight, no longer at the top of his
    game,
up against a nimble, invisible opponent, now down for the count.

III.

Bread

"Christ may have risen all at once, the gospel according to Betty Crocker seems to say, but flour and yeast and people made of dust require successive chances to reach their stature."
Garret Keizer

He takes the bread from the oven, pausing
midway between the bread board and cooling rack,
absorbing the gluteny scent through crusty skin
—the color of a child's arm
after a long hike on a summer's day.

She says, "I'll bring you a marvelous sourdough starter,
passed on to me from a cousin who ran a bakery—"
One pinch of starter travels two-thousand miles,
five hours through adventure, through altitude.
"It makes bread that Jesus would be proud to call body."

"Just a pinch?" she asks. "How can you deny me?"
She says that not to let her test it is tantamount to lack of love.
He gives in, just to see her face grow sanguine and lustful.

He once baked thirteen loaves for a homeless shelter;
then, nervous over numerology, he baked a fourteenth.
He couldn't remember which one had been the offending loaf,
so he started all over again. This time he scored each one
with a distinguishing mark using the blade of a sharp knife.

In the bread bowl, he mixes flour, water, salt.
Kneads, lets it ferment. Kneads again, pulling and folding,
folding and pulling, lets it come into fullness.
Then lifts it into the oven, from where it will emerge
so finely crusted, so evenly textured, so giving of itself.

Bread that cries, when placed in her mouth,
"Eat me and you will never die."

Intelligent Design

The knee is proof:
there's no such thing
as "intelligent design."
If there were, the knee
would be much improved,
rather than in need
of replacement.
The doctor tells me
they are doing
wonderful things
with technology these days,
have improved the joint
and bond—
Amazing, really, they
can take a sheep's tendon
and attach it there and here
or remove ligaments
from one part of the body,
secure it by drilling holes
and plugging them up,
stretching until taut
with tension superior
to the original.
The new designs
are so much better
("my better is better
than your better")
it seems obvious
the Creator
took off the afternoon
to play a round of golf
leaving the joint between
thigh bone and shin
to an intern.

Isn't it *obvious?*
I mean, 2 million years
of evolution haven't
improved the knee one whit.
Nothing intelligent about it.

Second Skin: A Sestina

In the yard by the barn was a snake
resting on a leaf-pile in the garden,
nearby his old shod skin
limp and lifeless under a noon-day sun.
Abandoned on the blades of grass,
like an untangled filament of memory.

The sight of him fired my memory,
which cast a shadow on the snake
(who now slithered away in the grass).
He lent a curious aspect to the garden—
aspect being its relation to the sun
—not unlike *his* relation to the skin.

He seemed to remember the skin.
(Do snakes *have* that much memory?)
Or was it a trick of the sun
that he mistook for a female snake?
When he made his way out of the garden,
I crept along quietly in the grass.

As I followed him there in the grass,
he stretched ever closer to the skin;
his path leading out of the garden,
as if tracing the line of a memory.
How strange, I thought, this snake,
disregarding the late summer sun.

Later, over-heated in afternoon sun,
I lay down to rest on the grass.
I watched again as the snake
tried to resuscitate his discarded skin,
perhaps to revive its dead memory
and lure it back home to the garden.

Cutting the lawn by the garden,
I must have been dizzy with sun,
or dozing in the haze of a memory.
Translucent flakes feathered the grass:
it was then I remembered the skin;
it was then I remembered the snake.

I sat by the garden dropping fresh-cut grass
onto my arm and its sun-baked skin,
clippings of memory snaking through my mind.

Redbud & Pitbull

The mining bees are emerging.
Males zipping around
tiny holes in the ground
where females are burrowing
beneath the redbud.
The males have a curious display;
more manic than romantic,
expecting a mate to think crazy
is sexy or superior.

I guess we all
fall prey
to a little crazy love
now and again,
do something foolish,
cross a line or two.
But the bees flying too close
to the ground are just frantic,
I can't imagine they'd make
suitable mates.

They course and dive and zip
(yes, that's the best word for it, *zip),*
while females wait below the redbud.
My pitbull Calvin watches
the mining bees swirling
above, around, and into the ground
beneath the redbud. He thinks,
Who or what are these (things)
buzzing and drilling in the dirt?

Truth is, the mining bees
—neither food nor friend—
pay him little interest.

Now Calvin grows bored,
slopes over to the sidewalk
flopping down in the sun.
The redbud's waxy leaves
glisten in the same sun,
green edging into red.

Calvin is mottled, piebald,
brindle and white with a big brown
eye patch that makes people smile.
He's a lover, not a fighter.
He cares little why the redbud's shock
of fuscia flowers, like scales or
a rash running up the limbs, hasn't shown.
He has no word for flowers
and little time for bees.

Calvin's Story

"Make it stop, make it stop,"
was all I kept thinking;
my eyes closed, some
bully biting my body, limbs,
tearing flesh and hair—
Boys pinned me to the pavement,
each one holding a leg, holding
me down on my back.
Another boy – so there were 5?
—pressing the bully into me
head lashing at anything
it could grab with canines.
I'm surprised I didn't black out—
Then, I remember a scuffle.
I was almost unconscious,
drifting in an out—
Two men freed my limbs,
but still I couldn't move.
One chased the boys
while the other lifted me,
cradled me, into a van.
I'll never forget the smell
—camphor, maybe, almost
lavender, medicinal.
The gentle one dabbed my
wounds with a wet cloth,
stroked me slowly, dabbed
—there was a lot of blood;
were there sirens? I don't
remember sirens. (Should
there have been sirens?)
The next thing I remember
is being on a cold, metal
table—a nurse or doctor

looking me over—another
shaking her head. The first
mumbles something (all I hear
is "Dog," that word they have
for us), then I'm sure she said,
"This one's a keeper, let's give
him a second chance…"
I wake in a crate, damp towel
beneath me, head swirling.
I must be in the "pound,"
there are others barking.
(I wish they would be quiet;
my head hurts.) Then
the pretty nurse or doctor
comes in, mumbles to me;
I look up, try to smile
(this seems to please her),
and I slip in and out of sleep.
                    Months later,
I'm sitting on a street corner,
leashed, with some of the nice pound
people. A lot of people pass by,
they pat my head, mumble
in that way they do, until one
couple lingers (a child or two
are with them, I can't recall).
They mumble to the pound people;
one of them (Alpha, I'll call him)
walks me; he has a firm hand,
but is gentle, in control.
Oh how I wish for a forever
family…but I don't
want to get my hopes up.
Then, the day is over,

back to the pound—sigh—
guess it wasn't meant to be.
Next night, however, there
is Alpha, and he's brought
some others. (Oh, let me be
on best behavior so they will
take me home.) They seem
to like when I snuggle, listen,
take commands, lick the cute
young ones—they are salty sweet!
Days go by after that night,
the pound people tell me
to get ready. Maybe, just maybe,
this is a good sign. Oh, I get so
excited my butt wiggles faster and
faster. Finally, the day comes;
Alpha arrives with the others,
and I think, *This is it*. I'm going home
with my forever family…to a home;
home at last for my second chance.

Passion

Devoid of passion, life's a mockery, really.
Like Shackleton's crew deprived of carbohydrates
surviving only on seal meat and penguin
those many months shipwrecked
in their quest for crossing over the frozen continent.
Yet we swim in it everyday. Hours drag;
no one breathes or forgets to breathe.
The net drags the unfrozen river,
but the bodies are cold, cold—
Are they frozen? Are we frozen?
We fall on our assets, as the fortunes fall.
We remain timid, perhaps a little gun shy.
Opportunities are lost at every turn.
We can not dive in for fear of getting—
Of getting what? Caught in the ice?
A broken leg or heart? The fracture will only
set if you let go; thaw comes only with friction.
What exactly are you waiting for?
Action is the basis of success.
As for passion, it can't be reasoned; only negotiated.
I'm digging in my heals; think there may be
a wire coming across explaining,
only no one knows the sender.

Listen, listen—LISTEN!

Firestorm

He sees the firestorm run across
her forehead like a lightning bolt
in 3D, and he knows she is going
to her dark place.

He rubs his thumb along that spot
where they say the 3rd eye
is found, and she looks at him
wondering how he knows.

They wait for the rain to stop
refill their coffee cups for
the 3rd time, not ready to leave,
knowing they can't yet stay—

He texts her from across the table.
It's the 3rd word that will stop her,
target of all his desire. He smiles
as the emoticon returns to her face.

Risks Are Risky

"Risks are risky; waiting is painful, indecision worse. If your heart tells you something, take it, relax and enjoy."
    Paulo Coelho

Risks are risky, stasis is static.
No one ever moved forward
who did not take a first step.
As we risk, we grow,
some would argue,
others would never leave
the house—too risky.
Ah, but the rewards—so sweet.
Risk is a probability
of specific eventualities,
resulting in an impact,
beneficial or adverse.
From the Arabic, *"rizk,"*
meaning "to seek prosperity,"
risk has inherent volatility
and unexpected variables.
It could be worse—
"Love is reckless," wrote Rumi.
"Reason seeks a profit."
Should we risk it all,
take a gamble, commit:
What gains! What possible returns!
Or hold back, cut loose at our stop-limit?
But what if it is the one opportunity,
the one investment that keeps giving;
that we have waited for all our lives?
We cannot know. But uncertainty
is risky too. The uncharted river
flows we know not where.
The river leads us onward,
but how can we know

what is around the bend:
oxbow or waterfall?
Or confluence: where two streams
come together to form a new river.
Even derivatives derive from *something*—
Whether in matters of romance or finance:
Risks are risky, but prosperity is thriving.

The Financial Suicides

Damned and damning are the fools,
their bald heads forgetful of sins.
Believing greed and graft are virtues,
they made all the rules,
spent lavishly on short-term views,
and made off with the most wins.

Masters of the Universe,
they excel at immoderation, going all-out,
but mastered neither failure nor humility.
Faced with losing everything or worse—
riches and status—they take the tidy,
albeit cowardly way out.

In the end, they come to find out
everything that man builds or begins
endures only for a moment.
Their legacies, without a doubt,
are consumed in the fires they foment
with their lies, deceit, and sins.

IV.

Becoming

Say that childhood memory
has more relevance than yesterday—

    a moose calf curled up against the side of a house

merely saying it may make it so.

The way a sunflower towers over a child,
each year growing shorter—

    a hermit crab crawling out of a coconut

—no, the child growing taller.

    a sharp-shinned hawk swooping over a stubble field

imagining the earth, "the earth is all before me,"
blossoming as it stretches to the sun—

    a brilliant red eft—baby salamander—held aloft in a small,

  pink hand

Is home the mother's embrace?

    a white cabbage butterfly flitting atop purple flox

The child sees his world or hers

stroking the furry back of a bumblebee

head full of seed, until it droops,
spent, ready to sow the seeds.

Say that our presence in the world

a millipede curling up at the child's slightest touch

is making the book of our becoming.

Redshifting

A crow makes its call from a distant tree,
rain soaking the meadow, soaking the earth.

An oak leaf cutting through the air
slicing from branch to ground.

The universe expanding in space-time,
with little regard for the matter in its way—

A star in the night sky redshifting (did you see it?)
as the eye adjusts, from blue to green to yellow to red.

Object radiating light, moving away from us,
light waves becoming longer, less energetic,

red heart pulsing, wavelength of lower frequency
then blue heart, pulsing out longing—

Crow flies overhead, cawing, its frequency,
its pitch, becoming higher when approaching,

then lower, longer, as it passes, until distance
makes the heart's pitch lower, too, with absence.

Absence, a lower frequency than presence.
Say that the heart redshifts down as it reflects light.

Distance, the time it takes love to travel from star to star,
lover to loved. Love is not a vacuum,

its waves bend with its expansion,
the heart is as that red star in a field of blue.

We cannot know its origin or its destination,
but if we think about that place or that absence,
we are already there:

redshifting through the distance of space-time or
blueshifting, where frequency and proximity collide.

Shapeshifting

"When young Dawn with her rose-red fingers shone once more..."
Homer

Give the night back to the night,
the stars back to the sky—

Give the earth, spinning in space,
back to the earth—

        (the stars look black tonight)

Give the moon, no, keep the moon,
it is the stars we want to give back—

Give the soil back to the isopod
emerging to the surface

        (what is it looking for?)

Give the Dawn back her rose-red fingers,
she needs them more than the night.

Give the blue jay back his morning,
taken from him by the chickadee—

        (sounds are deeper in solitude)

Give back to the sunshine
what darkness is his—

Give back to the night
what light is hers—

       (stars, moon, clouds—)

Shape-shifting: blue jay into chickadee
into blue jay, night into day

into—what?

      ("Harassed unrest"?)

Give back to the earth what is hers,
she will forgive you for taking it

or she will turn into a wolf.

Healing

"Healing, not saving."
  Gary Snyder

Keep warm. Sun following
rain; rain following drought.

Perhaps we have come far enough
along in this world to start

healing, protecting from harm,
from our disjunctive lives.

The way the skin repairs with a scab,
injury mediated by mindfulness.

The bark of the "tree of blood"
heals wounds we cannot see.

Deliver us from the time of trial
and save us from ourselves.

Cultivating (Preserving)

Dwelling as preserving
is cultivating.
Dwelling means knowing
what inhabits a place
and understanding that
which *belongs* to a place.

We cultivate what grows,
while building things
that don't grow.
We seek the organic
in our own creations,
which are inorganic.

Imposing our will
on the landscape,
we can remove either
that which promotes capacity
or that which prevents capacity.

We are tenders of the garden,
we tend what needs tending
(heart or "langscape")

What we save remains—

Mapping

"More delicate than the historians' are the map-makers' colors."
Elizabeth Bishop

A boundary is where something begins,
spaces formed by locations.
Mapping is building spaces
and locations, as it is made.

Nature's boundaries
defined by interconnections,
and geophysical fact
not geopolitical friction—

Aspect, climate, elevation,
land forms and bodies of water,
aggregation of species,
watershed divides,
soil, time, bedrock, strata,
and shifting—

of this we are certain:
boundaries are always shifting.
(Only Man tries to deny this,
imposing order where chaos rules.)

Say that boundaries
are the beginning,
where things start,
not the end-point;
say boundaries are a beginning,
one among many.

Running

"Not beauty, or ugliness, either, but a disturbing kind of satisfaction."
  Philip Johnson

Think of a watershed as a river's neighborhood;
the running stream, a kind of architecture—

Find the stream that forms the watershed in which you live;
hear the water running (if it is frozen, listen through the ice).

The architect finds such harmony
in the precise moment a corner is designed—
tension, productivity, and grace.

Hear it? Running water, then silence, then water running.

The architect Frank Gehry achieves
a "double sense of space"; like a watershed,
his buildings are formed by what flows in *and* out—

Follow the stream, run the watershed,
chase the flash-and-glamour of fish scales
underwater: spawning entire new dynamics of space.

The way a storm moving through a valley
redirects energy back into a stream.

Gehry asked himself, "Why not do fish?"
A lasting design, form linked to function.

So he did fish. Fish scale chairs, fish lamps.
And then buildings, buildings
that seemed to swim around their own corners, seemed to spawn.

Scale the banks, river walls, riverrun
—erosion and construction—

titanium trapezoids billowing at the end of Bilbao's streets,
more like spun-sugar than shaped metal.

Run the river toward *something.*
There's tension in productivity and grace.

Perhaps this double sense of space is sense of place:
No matter where we are, we are always in a watershed.

Presencing

"A space must be maintained or desire ends."
  Anne Carson

The scent of your presence evaporates desire,
the space between you and we, between otherness—

becoming the presence of another's absence;
weight of earth spinning its matter apart, weight

of our *becoming,* our *presencing.*
At present, the time between past and future—

"this very time that is space, this very space that is time."
Vanishing space that surrounds us, space of intimacy;

a collarbone caressed by a tongue, hair flowing over hipbones—
scent of your presence lingering, trapping memory in a lifetime,

an infinite solitude. Solitude the presence of absence:
scent of a fox long after the fox is gone—

                    II.
Presence, essence, *esse, in esse:* in view.
Absence, *abesse:* to be away.

abesse, esse, inter*esse:* absence leads to interest in presence, hence
    desire

                    of a lover
                    of another
                    of an Other
                    of one

84

of you
of what one holds near
nearness
holds dear
dearness
abesse
absence
desir

desiderāre: to regret the absence of, not to regress, go back, but
    to regret, to re-greet (to greet again?).

    III.
The nearness of you
evaporates absence,
as presence evaporates absence,
essence remains, hence desire—
your presencing becomes
your absence, your essence.

Indwelling

Shooting stars cross the city's night sky.
In the moment before they fall, think about dwellings,

houses made of brick, stone, and wood—dwelling and indwelling
miracle keeping matter together, from imploding or inverting.

How dwellings *become* a city, interdependent.
How stars *become* a night sky, suspended.

(Late Fall, nearly winter, fog-caul warms night air through
    inversion.
The meteor version of life heads straight to the matter of our bed.)

What holds up the sky holds each one of us, too—
as we move against one another in this taut, elastic field,

warming with each movement, causing little inversions
all around us, and shooting stars—

V.

The Poet Gene

The gene for "poet" has likely been isolated,
somewhere in a lab in southern California.
And I wonder how close it is to the gene
that makes you crave potato chips
or the "coffee-drinker" gene, perhaps,
or the one that causes procrastination.
If they have the poet gene cornered
in a Petri dish, will they admonish it
for all the bad poems ever written,
however unwittingly?

Would it improve the human
to have the poet gene spliced
into fruit or beef – or even bacon?
Poetry-enhanced bacon. Now *that's*
genetic modification one can get behind!

What if this innocent experiment turned wicked?
Oh, but what if it went "aft agley"?
Think of it, more bad poems by more bad poets—
(Increased productivity isn't always a good thing.)
Perhaps *this* poem is, in fact, one of them,
a mutated, altered, monster poem
waiting to grab you by the throat and…*Ahem.*

Think of the sheer volume of bad poetry
overtaking the world, smothering us;
entire forests decimated for paper
upon which these poems are printed
or hundreds of iPhone apps built
to accommodate a staggering number of poems
cranked out by "GMPs" (genetically modified poets)
careering and MFAing all over the place.

Undoubtedly, someone will decide to splice
the poet gene from one poet into another. Then what?
Talk about trouble: one side striving for simplicity;
the other deliberately obtuse and indirect.

No, best leave the poet gene out of even this poem;
rather, focus on how to make potato chip consumption
actually slimming to the human figure, especially
when consumed with large quantities of your favorite ale
and generous servings of *bacon.*

The Postlude, or How I Became a Poet

"What dwelling shall receive me?...The earth is all before me."
  Wordsworth, "The Prelude"

I am a child, crawling around in the leaves
With Gladys Taylor while she names the trees,
parts the grasses, digs into the earth with a gardener's trowel.
She picks out worms and slugs, millipedes
And springtails, which we see with a "Berlese funnel."
Busy decomposers working their busy tasks,
Turning waste into energy, leaf litter into soil again.
Gladys names things for me: "That oak,
That maple there, that sassafras, smell its roots."
                        "Root beer," I exclaim,
Her laughter peeling away into the hills. Later,
With Comstock's *Handbook of Nature Study*
On the table next to the unending jigsaw puzzle,
Gladys opens to "The Oaks," reading or reciting:
"The symbol of strength since man first gazed
Upon its noble proportions..." Then she sings Virgil,

>   *Full in the midst of his own strength he stands*
>   *Stretching his brawny arms and leafy hands,*
>   *His shade protects the plains, his head the hills commands.*

Leaves and acorns spread across the table,
Each divided to its source, as if cataloguing specimens:
The white and chestnut oaks, red and scarlet,
Every oak in the neighborhood, sketching the leaves,
Tracing and coloring them. Then questions, such questions:
"Where did we see this one growing?" "How tall?"
"Are the branches crooked or straight?"
"Round leaves or pointy?"

91

                    And then a game of matching
Acorn to leaf; a most difficult lesson—as difficult
As those jigsaw puzzles for a boy lacking patience
Or attention. Outdoors again, to *learn* attention,
Naming the birds that came to eat at the feeder:
Chickadee, sparrow, nuthatch, tufted titmouse,
The ubiquitous jay.
                    "The mockingbird, hear
How he makes fun of all the other birds." Now
Thrasher, now robin, the *sweet sweet sweet,*
Very merry cheer of the song sparrow,
Or the flicker's *whicka whicka wick-a-wick.*
Then a jay's piercing caw, a cat's meow,
This was all the mocker's doing! And wide-eyed,
I stare, as Gladys seems to call birds to her side.
"The robin tells us when it's going to rain,
Not just when spring is come," she says. "Look
How he sings as he waits for worms to surface."

        That summer, rowing around the pond
By Brookfield's floating bridge, I saw a beaver
Slap the water with its tail, and then swim around the boat,
As if in warning. Under water a moment later he went,
Only to appear twenty yards away, scrambling up the bank,
Back to his busy work. *"Busy as a beaver,"* Gladys laughs.
Then a serious tone, "You know that beavers gathered
The mud with which the earth was made?"
(I later learned this was Indian legend; to her
There was little difference among the ways of knowing.)
All around the pond the beavers made of the creek,
The sharp points of their handiwork: birches broken
For succulent shoots, twigs, leaves and bark bared.

"When they hear running water, they've just got
To get back to work!" Beavers moving across
The water, noses up, branches in their teeth,
Building or repairing dams or adding to their lodges,
Lodges that look like huts Indians might have used.
I watched for them—beavers and Indians—when
Out on the water, and once I remember a beaver
Jumping clear out of the water over the bow of the rowboat!
Later, wading in the mud shallows by the pond's pebbly edge,
I came out of the water to find leeches covering my feet,
Filling the spaces between my toes. Screaming, fascinated,
I learned that they sucked blood, little bloodsuckers,
A kind of worm, which were once used to reduce fever.

        That was me to Gladys Taylor's teaching,
Wanting to soak up everything she had to give me.
We picked pea pods out of the garden, shelled
On the spot, our thumbs a sort prying-spoon,
And ate blackberries by the bushel or bellyful,
Probably blueberries, too, I don't know. And
Seeing the milkweed grown fat with its milk,
I popped it open, squirting the white viscous
Juice at my brother. Gladys always found
A caterpillar on the milkweed leaves, tiger stripes
Of black, white, and yellow. "Monarchs," she said,
"The most beautiful butterfly you'll ever see."
I looked incredulously at the caterpillar, believing,
Because she was Gladys, but not believing her,
That this wiggly, worm-like thing could be a butterfly.
Later, she found a chrysalis and took the leaf
And twig from which it hung. She placed it atop
A jar on the picnic table, and each day we waited

—waited for what? I didn't know. Until one day,
It was empty, a hollow, blue-green emerald shell,
And I almost cried. "Look, out in the meadow,"
She instructed. Hundreds, it seemed like
Thousands, of monarch butterflies flitting about,
From flower to flower!
                              The wooly-bear
Was easier to study. We put it in a jar with a twig
And fresh grass every day; it curled and slept and ate
Until one day it climbed, climbed to the top
Of the twig and spun a cocoon from its own hairs.
There it stayed for weeks, until at last I thought it dead.
But then, emerging from its silky capsule, a hideous sight:
Gray, tawny, dull--a tiger moth! Nothing like the cute
And fuzzy reddish-brown and black teddy bear we'd found.
"This is magic," said Gladys. "*Nature's magic*."

And I believed her, believe her still, that there is some magic
In nature speaking within us when we are in it, *of it,* let it in—
Science may explain this all away, physics or biology,
But nothing will shake my faith in this:
That the force of nature, the inner fire, *anima mundi,*
Gaia, or whatever you may call it, is alive within each
Being and everything with which we share this earth.

   My Mother Earth was Gladys Taylor, and she
Taught me these things, and about poetry and art,
In the few, brief years we had together. Gladys
Taught me how to look at the world—to pay attention.
Thus began my education from Nature's bosom:
A woman, childless herself (I believe) who,
In her dungarees and work-shirt, took a child
Under her wing and gave him *gold,*
Gave him his desire for dwelling on this earth.

About the Author

Scott Edward Anderson has been a Concordia Fellow at the Millay Colony for the Arts, and received both the *Nebraska Review* Award and the Aldrich Emerging Poets Award. His poetry has appeared in the *Alaska Quarterly Review, American Poetry Review, Anon, The Cortland Review, CrossConnect, Earth's Daughters, Isotope, La Petite Zine, Many Mountains Moving, Nebraska Review, Poetica, River Oak Review, Slant* and *Terrain,* among other publications. He was a founding editor of *Ducky Magazine,* writes "The Green Skeptic" blog (TheGreenSkeptic.com), and blogs about poetry at seapoetry.wordpress.com. Anderson is also the author of *Walks in Nature's Empire* (The Countryman Press, 1995).